Selected Poems

Thom Gunn

Selected Poems
1950–1975

Farrar Straus Giroux / New York

Copyright © 1957, 1958, 1961, 1967, 1971, 1973, 1974,
1975, 1976, 1979 by Thom Gunn
All rights reserved
First American printing, 1979
Printed in the United States of America
Designed by Constance Fogler

Library of Congress Cataloging in Publication Data
Gunn, Thom. Selected poems, 1950–1975.
PR6013.U65A6 1979   821'.9'14   79–9158

Contents

I

The Wound

The huge wound in my head began to heal
About the beginning of the seventh week.
Its valleys darkened, its villages became still:
For joy I did not move and dared not speak,
Not doctors would cure it, but time, its patient skill.

And constantly my mind returned to Troy.
After I sailed the seas I fought in turn
On both sides, sharing even Helen's joy
Of place, and growing up—to see Troy burn—
As Neoptolemus, that stubborn boy.

I lay and rested as prescription said.
Maneuvered with the Greeks, or sallied out
Each day with Hector. Finally my bed
Became Achilles' tent, to which the lout
Thersites came reporting numbers dead.

I was myself: subject to no man's breath:
My own commander was my enemy.
And while my belt hung up, sword in the sheath,
Thersites shambled in and breathlessly
Cackled about my friend Patroclus' death.

I called for armor, rose, and did not reel.
But, when I thought, rage at his noble pain
Flew to my head, and turning I could feel
My wound break open wide. Over again
I had to let those storm-lit valleys heal.

(3)

Wind in the Street

The same faces, and then the same scandals
Confront me inside the talking shop which I
Frequent for my own good. So the assistant
Points to the old cogwheels, the old handles
Set in machines which to buy would be to buy
The same faces, and then the same scandals.

I climb by the same stairs to a square attic.
And I gasp, for surely this is something new!
So square, so simple. It is new to be so simple.
Then I see the same sky through the skylight, static
Cloudless, the same artificial toylike blue.
The same stairs led to the same attic.

I only came, I explain, to look round,
To the assistant who coos while I regain the street.
Searching thoroughly, I did not see what I wanted.
What I wanted would have been what I found.
My voice carries, his voice blows to his feet:
I only came, I explain, to look round.

I may return, meanwhile I'll look elsewhere:
My want may modify to what I have seen.
So I smile wearily, though even as I smile
A purposeful gust of wind tugs at my hair;
But I turn, I wave, I am not sure what I mean.
I may return, meanwhile I'll look elsewhere.

Round and Round

The lighthouse keeper's world is round,
Belongings skipping in a ring—
All that a man may want, therein,
A wife, a wireless, bread, jam, soap,
Yet day by night his straining hope
Shoots out to live upon the sound
The spinning waves make while they break
For their own endeavor's sake—
The lighthouse keeper's world is round.

He wonders, winding up the stair
To work the lamp which lights the ships,
Why each secured possession skips
With face towards the center turned,
From table-loads of books has learned
Shore-worlds are round as well, not square,
But there things dance with faces out-
ward turned: faces of fear and doubt?
He wonders, winding up the stair.

When it is calm, the rocks are safe
To take a little exercise
But all he does is fix his eyes
On that huge totem he has left
Where thoughts dance round what will not shift—
His secret inarticulate grief.
Waves have no sun, but are beam-caught
Running below his feet, wry salt,
When, in a calm, the rocks are safe.

Lazarus Not Raised

He was not changed. His friends around the grave
Stared down upon his greasy placid face
Bobbing on shadows; nothing it seemed could save
His body now from the sand below their wave,
The scheduled miracle not taking place.

He lay inert beneath those outstretched hands
Which beckoned him to life. Though coffin case
Was ready to hold life and winding bands
At his first stir would loose the frozen glands,
The scheduled miracle did not take place.

O Lazarus, distended body laid
Glittering without weight on death's surface,
Rise now before you sink, we dare not wade
Into that sad marsh where (the mourners cried)
The scheduled miracle cannot take place.

When first aroused and given thoughts and breath
He chose to amble at an easy pace
In childhood fields imaginary and safe—
Much like the trivial territory of death
(The miracle had not yet taken place).

He chose to spend his thoughts like this at first
And disregard the nag of offered grace,
Then chose to spend the rest of them in rest.
The final effort came, forward we pressed
To see the scheduled miracle take place:

Abruptly the corpse blinked and shook his head
Then sank again, sliding without a trace
From sight, to take slime on the deepest bed
Of vacancy. He had chosen to stay dead,
The scheduled miracle did not take place.

Nothing else changed. I saw somebody peer,
Stooping, into the oblong box of space.
His friends had done their best: without such fear,
Without that terrified awakening glare,
The scheduled miracle would have taken place.

Looking Glass

Remote, it lives now in a tiny glass,
Charmed-still forever at one stage of growing:
Trees are in leaf, and children all day long
Laugh in their effortless continual going
To hidden ends along the ways of grass,
And birds make great perspectives of their song.

I still hold Eden in my garden wall.
It was not innocence lost, not innocence
But a fine callous fickleness which could fix
On every novelty the mind or sense
Reached for, gratification being all,
And closed the tool box for the box of tricks.

I am the gardener now myself, and know,
Though I am free to leave the path and tear
Ripe from the branch the yellows and the reds,
I am responsible for order here
(The time it takes to teach the fruits to grow,
The pains of keeping neat the flower beds).

What little watering I do is pleasure,
I let the birds on pear and apple sup,
I do not use my clippers or my rake,
I do not tie the fallen branches up,
I leave the weeding and employ my leisure
In idling on the lawns or by the lake.

Gardening manuals frown at this neglect
But risks are authorized by such a weather.
What want but water should the flowers need?
I will enjoy the green before it wither,
And do not care if villagers suspect
It goes to seed. How well it goes to seed . . .

I see myself inside a looking glass
Framed there by shadowed trees alive with song
And fruits no sooner noticed than enjoyed;
I take it from my pocket and gaze long,
Forgetting in my pleasure how I pass
From town to town, damp-booted, unemployed.

Tamer and Hawk

I thought I was so tough,
But gentled at your hands,
Cannot be quick enough
To fly for you and show
That when I go I go
At your commands.

Even in flight above
I am no longer free:
You seeled me with your love,
I am blind to other birds—
The habit of your words
Has hooded me.

As formerly, I wheel
I hover and I twist,
But only want the feel,
In my possessive thought,
Of catcher and of caught
Upon your wrist.

You but half civilize,
Taming me in this way.
Through having only eyes
For you I fear to lose,
I lose to keep, and choose
Tamer as prey.

The Beach Head

Now that a letter gives me ground at last
For starting from, I see my enterprise
Is more than application by a blast
Upon a trumpet slung beside a gate,
Security a fraud, and how unwise
Was disembarking on your Welfare State.

What should they see in you but what I see,
These friends you mention whom I do not know?
—You unsuspecting that a refugee
Might want the land complete, write in a tone
Too matter-of-fact of small affairs below
A minister's seduction of the Crown.

And even if they could be innocent,
They still applaud you, keep you satisfied
And occupy your time, which I resent.
Their werewolf lust and cunning are afraid
Of night exposure in the hair, so hide
Distant as possible from my palisade.

I have my ground. A brain-sick enemy
Pacing his beach head he so plotted for
Which now seems trivial to his jealousy
And ignorance of the great important part,
I almost wish I had no narrow shore.
I seek a pathway to the country's heart.

Shall I be John a Gaunt and with my band
Of mad bloods pass in one spectacular dash,
Fighting before and after, through your land,
To issue out unharmed the farther side,
With little object other than panache
And showing what great odds may be defied?

That way achievement would at once be history:
Living inside, I would not know the danger:
Hurry is blind and so does not brave mystery;
I should be led to underrate, by haste,
Your natural beauties: while I, hare-brained stranger,
Would not be much distinguished from the rest.

Or shall I wait and calculate my chances
Consolidating this my inch-square base,
—Myself a spy, killing your spies-in-glances—
Planning when you have least supplies or clothing
A pincer move to end in an embrace,
And risk that your mild liking turn to loathing?

II

On the Move

The blue jay scuffling in the bushes follows
Some hidden purpose, and the gust of birds
That spurts across the field, the wheeling swallows,
Have nested in the trees and undergrowth.
Seeking their instinct, or their poise, or both,
One moves with an uncertain violence
Under the dust thrown by a baffled sense
Or the dull thunder of approximate words.

On motorcycles, up the road, they come:
Small, black, as flies hanging in heat, the Boys,
Until the distance throws them forth, their hum
Bulges to thunder held by calf and thigh.
In goggles, donned impersonality,
In gleaming jackets trophied with the dust,
They strap in doubt—by hiding it, robust—
And almost hear a meaning in their noise.

Exact conclusion of their hardiness
Has no shape yet, but from known whereabouts
They ride, direction where the tires press.
They scare a flight of birds across the field:
Much that is natural, to the will must yield.
Men manufacture both machine and soul,
And use what they imperfectly control
To dare a future from the taken routes.

It is a part solution, after all.
One is not necessarily discord
On earth; or damned because, half animal,
One lacks direct instinct, because one wakes
Afloat on movement that divides and breaks.
One joins the movement in a valueless world,
Choosing it, till, both hurler and the hurled,
One moves as well, always toward, toward.

A minute holds them, who have come to go:
The self-defined, astride the created will
They burst away; the towns they travel through
Are home for neither bird nor holiness,
For birds and saints complete their purposes.
At worst, one is in motion; and at best,
Reaching no absolute, in which to rest,
One is always nearer by not keeping still.

California

The Unsettled Motorcyclist's Vision of His Death

Across the open countryside,
Into the walls of rain I ride.
It beats my cheek, drenches my knees,
But I am being what I please.

The firm heath stops, and marsh begins.
Now we're at war: whichever wins
My human will cannot submit
To nature, though brought out of it.
The wheels sink deep; the clear sound blurs:
Still, bent on the handlebars,
I urge my chosen instrument
Against the mere embodiment.
The front wheel wedges fast between
Two shrubs of glazed insensate green
—Gigantic order in the rim
Of each flat leaf. Black eddies brim
Around my heel which, pressing deep,
Accelerates the waiting sleep.

I used to live in sound, and lacked
Knowledge of still or creeping fact,
But now the stagnant strips my breath,
Leant on my cheek in weight of death.
Though so oppressed I find I may
Through substance move. I pick my way,
Where death and life in one combine,
Through the dark earth that is not mine,
Crowded with fragments, blunt, unformed;

While past my ear where noises swarmed
The marsh plant's white extremities,
Slow without patience, spread at ease
Invulnerable and soft, extend
With a quiet grasping toward their end.

And though the tubers, once I rot,
Reflesh my bones with pallid knot,
Till swelling out my clothes they feign
This dummy is a man again,
It is as servants they insist,
Without volition that they twist;
And habit does not leave them tired,
By men laboriously acquired.
Cell after cell the plants convert
My special richness in the dirt:
All that they get, they get by chance.

And multiply in ignorance.

First Meeting with a Possible Mother-in-Law

She thought, without the benefit of knowing,
You, who had been hers, were not any more.
We had locked our love in to leave nothing showing
From the room her handiwork had crammed before;
But—much revealing in its figured sewing—
A piece of stuff hung out, caught in the door.
I caused the same suspicion I watched growing:
Who could not tell what whole the part stood for?

There was small likeness between her and me:
Two strangers left upon a bare top landing,
I for a prudent while, she totally.

But, eyes turned from the bright material hint,
Each shared too long a second's understanding,
Learning the other's terms of banishment.

High Fidelity

I play your furies back to me at night,
The needle dances in the grooves they made,
For fury is passion like love, and fury's bite,
These grooves, no sooner than a love mark fade;
Then all swings round to nightmare: from the rim,
To prove the guilt I don't admit by day,
I duck love as a witch to sink or swim
Till in the ringed and level I survey
The tuneless circles that succeed a voice.
They run, without distinction, passion, rage,
Around a soloist's merely printed name
That still turns, from the impetus not choice,
Surrounded in that played-out pose of age
By notes he was, but cannot be again.

Autumn Chapter in a Novel

Through woods, Mme Une Telle, a trifle ill
With idleness, but no less beautiful,
Walks with the young tutor, round their feet
Mob syllables slurred to a fine complaint,
Which in their time held off the natural heat.

The sun is distant, and they fill out space
Sweatless as watercolor under glass.
He kicks abruptly. But we may suppose
The leaves he scatters thus will settle back
In much the same position as they rose.

A tutor's indignation works on air,
Altering nothing; action bustles where,
Towards the pool by which they lately stood,
The husband comes discussing with his bailiff
Poachers, the broken fences round the wood.

Pighead! The poacher is at large, and lingers,
A dead mouse gripped between his sensitive fingers:
Fences already keep the live game out:
See how your property twists her parasol,
Hesitates in the tender trap of doubt.

Here they repair, here daily handle lightly
The brief excitements that disturb them nightly;
Sap draws back inch by inch, and to the ground
The words they uttered rustle constantly:
Silent, they watch the growing, weightless mound.

They leave at last a chosen element,
Resume the motions of their discontent;
She takes her sewing up, and he again
Names to her son the deserts on the globe,
And leaves thrust violently upon the pane.

The Silver Age

Do not inquire from the centurion nodding
At the corner, with his head gentle over
The swelling breastplate, where true Rome is found.
Even of Livy there are volumes lost.
All he can do is guide you through the moonlight.

When he moves, mark how his eager striding,
To which we know the darkness is a river
Sullen with mud, is easy as on ground.
We know it is a river never crossed
By any but some few who hate the moonlight.

And when he speaks, mark how his ancient wording
Is hard with indignation of a lover.
"I do not think our new Emperor likes the sound
Of turning squadrons or the last post.
Consorts with Christians, I think he lives in moonlight."

Hurrying to show you his companions guarding,
He grips your arm like a cold strap of leather,
Then halts, earthpale, as he stares round and round.
What made this one fragment of a sunken coast
Remain, far out, to be beaten by the moonlight?

At the Back of the North Wind

All summer's warmth was stored there in the hay;
Below, the troughs of water froze: the boy
Climbed nightly up the rungs behind the stalls
And planted deep between the clothes he heard
The kind wind bluster, but the last he knew
Was sharp and filled his head, the smell of hay.

Here wrapped within the cobbled mews he woke.
Passing from summer, climbing down through winter
He broke into an air that kept no season:
Denying change, for it was always there.
It nipped the memory numb, scalding away
The castle of winter and the smell of hay.

The ostlers knew, but did not tell him more
Than hay is what we turn to. Other smells,
Horses, leather, manure, fresh sweat, and sweet
Mortality, he found them on the North.
That was her sister, East, that shrilled all day
And swept the mews dead clean from wisps of hay.

In Praise of Cities

I

Indifferent to the indifference that conceived her,
Grown buxom in disorder now, she accepts
—Like dirt, strangers, or moss upon her churches—
Your tribute to the wharf of circumstance,
Rejected side street, formal monument . . .
And, irresistible, the thoroughfare.

You welcome in her what remains of you;
And what is strange and what is incomplete
Compels a passion without understanding,
For all you cannot be.

I I

            Only at dawn
You might escape, she sleeps then for an hour:
Watch where she hardly breathes, spread out and cool,
Her pavements desolate in the dim dry air.

I I I

You stay. Yet she is occupied, apart.
Out of a mist the river turns to see
Whether you follow still. You stay. At evening
Your blood gains pace even as her blood does.

IV

Casual yet urgent in her lovemaking,
She constantly asserts her independence:
Suddenly turning moist pale walls upon you
—Your own designs, peeling and unachieved—
Or her whole darkness hunching in an alley.
And all at once you enter the embrace
Withheld by day while you solicited.
She wanders lewdly, whispering her given name,
Charing Cross Road, or Forty-second Street:
The longest streets, desire that never ends,
Familiar and inexplicable, wearing
Cosmetic light a fool could penetrate.
She presses you with her hard ornaments,
Arcades, late movie shows, the piled lit windows
Of surplus stores. Here she is loveliest;
Extreme, material, and the work of man.

Jesus and His Mother

My only son, more God's than mine,
Stay in this garden ripe with pears.
The yielding of their substance wears
A modest and contented shine:
And when they weep with age, not brine
But lazy syrup are their tears.
"I am my own and not my own."

He seemed much like another man,
That silent foreigner who trod
Outside my door with lily rod:
How could I know what I began
Meeting the eyes more furious than
The eyes of Joseph, those of God?
I was my own and not my own.

And who are these twelve laboring men?
I do not understand your words:
I taught you speech, we named the birds,
You marked their big migrations then
Like any child. So turn again
To silence from the place of crowds.
"I am my own and not my own."

Why are you sullen when I speak?
Here are your tools, the saw and knife
And hammer on your bench. Your life
Is measured here in week and week
Planed as the furniture you make,

And I will teach you like a wife
To be my own and all my own.

Who like an arrogant wind blown
Where he may please, needs no content?
Yet I remember how you went
To speak with scholars in furred gown.
I hear an outcry in the town;
Who carries that dark instrument?
"One all his own and not his own."

Treading the green and nimble sward
I stare at a strange shadow thrown.
Are you the boy I bore alone,
No doctor near to cut the cord?
I cannot reach to call you Lord,
Answer me as my only son.
"I am my own and not my own."

To Yvor Winters, 1955

I leave you in your garden.

In the yard
Behind it, run the Airedales you have reared
With boxer's vigilance and poet's rigor:
Dog generations you have trained the vigor
That few can breed to train and fewer still
Control with the deliberate human will.
And in the house there rest, piled shelf on shelf,
The accumulations that compose the self—
Poem and history: for if we use
Words to maintain the actions that we choose,
Our words, with slow defining influence,
Stay to mark out our chosen lineaments.

Continual temptation waits on each
To renounce his empire over thought and speech,
Till he submit his passive faculties
To evening, come where no resistance is;
The unmotivated sadness of the air
Filling the human with his own despair.
Where now lies power to hold the evening back?
Implicit in the gray is total black:
Denial of the discriminating brain
Brings the neurotic vision, and the vein
Of necromancy. All as relative
For mind as for the sense, we have to live
In a half world, not ours nor history's,
And learn the false from half-true premises.

But sitting in the dusk—though shapes combine,
Vague mass replacing edge and flickering line,
You keep both Rule and Energy in view,
Much power in each, most in the balanced two:
Ferocity existing in the fence
Built by an exercised intelligence.
Though night is always close, complete negation
Ready to drop on wisdom and emotion,
Night from the air or the carnivorous breath,
Still it is right to know the force of death,
And, as you do, persistent, tough in will,
Raise from the excellent the better still.

The Corridor

A separate place between the thought and felt
The empty hotel corridor was dark.
But here the keyhole shone, a meaning spark.
What fires were latent in it! So he knelt.

Now, at the corridor's much lighter end,
A pier glass hung upon the wall and showed,
As by an easily deciphered code,
Dark, door, and man, hooped by a single band.

He squinted through the keyhole, and within
Surveyed an act of love that frank as air
He was too ugly for, or could not dare,
Or at a crucial moment thought a sin.

Pleasure was simple thus: he mastered it.
If once he acted as participant
He would be mastered, the inhabitant
Of someone else's world, mere shred to fit.

He moved himself to get a better look
And then it was he noticed in the glass
Two strange eyes in a fascinated face
That watched him like a picture in a book.

The instant drove simplicity away—
The scene was altered, it depended on
His kneeling, when he rose they were clean gone
The couple in the keyhole; this would stay.

For if the watcher of the watcher shown
There in the distant glass should be watched too,
Who can be master, free of others; who
Can look around and say he is alone?

Moreover, who can know that what he sees
Is not distorted, that he is not seen
Distorted by a pier glass, curved and lean?
Those curious eyes, through him, were linked to these—

These lovers altered in the cornea's bend.
What could he do but leave the keyhole, rise,
Holding those eyes as equal in his eyes,
And go, one hand held out, to meet a friend?

Vox Humana

Being without quality
I appear to you at first
as an unkempt smudge, a blur,
an indefinite haze, mere-
ly pricking the eyes, almost
nothing. Yet you perceive me.

I have been always most close
when you had least resistance,
falling asleep, or in bars;
during the unscheduled hours,
though strangely without substance,
I hang, there and ominous.

Aha, sooner or later
you will have to name me, and,
as you name, I shall focus,
I shall become more precise.
O Master (for you command
in naming me, you prefer)!

I was, for Alexander,
the certain victory; I
was hemlock for Socrates;
and, in the dry night, Brutus
waking before Philippi
stopped me, crying out, "Caesar!"

Or if you call me the blur
that in fact I am, you shall
yourself remain blurred, hanging
like smoke indoors. For you bring,
to what you define now, all
there is, ever, of future.

III

In Santa Maria del Popolo

Waiting for when the sun an hour or less
Conveniently oblique makes visible
The painting on one wall of this recess
By Caravaggio, of the Roman School,
I see how shadow in the painting brims
With a real shadow, drowning all shapes out
But a dim horse's haunch and various limbs,
Until the very subject is in doubt.

But evening gives the act, beneath the horse
And one indifferent groom, I see him sprawl,
Foreshortened from the head, with hidden face,
Where he has fallen, Saul becoming Paul.
O wily painter, limiting the scene
From a cacophony of dusty forms
To the one convulsion, what is it you mean
In that wide gesture of the lifting arms?

No Ananias croons a mystery yet,
Casting the pain out under name of sin.
The painter saw what was, an alternate
Candor and secrecy inside the skin.
He painted, elsewhere, that firm insolent
Young whore in Venus' clothes, those pudgy cheats,
Those sharpers; and was strangled, as things went,
For money, by one such picked off the streets.

I turn, hardly enlightened, from the chapel
To the dim interior of the church instead,
In which there kneel already several people,
Mostly old women: each head closeted
In tiny fists holds comfort as it can.
Their poor arms are too tired for more than this
—For the large gesture of solitary man,
Resisting, by embracing, nothingness.

From the Highest Camp

Nothing in this bright region melts or shifts.
The local names are concepts: the Ravine,
Pemmican Ridge, North Col, Death Camp, they mean
The streetless rise, the dazzling abstract drifts,
To which particular names adhere by chance,
From custom lightly, not from character.
We stand on a white terrace and confer;
This is the last camp of experience.

What is that sudden yelp upon the air?
And whose are these cold droppings? whose malformed
Purposeless tracks about the slope? We know.
The abominable endures, existing where
Nothing else can: it is—unfed, unwarmed—
Born of rejection, of the boundless snow.

Innocence

for Tony White

He ran the course and as he ran he grew,
And smelt his fragrance in the field. Already,
Running he knew the most he ever knew,
The egotism of a healthy body.

Ran into manhood, ignorant of the past:
Culture of guilt and guilt's vague heritage,
Self-pity and the soul; what he possessed
Was rich, potential, like the bud's tipped rage.

The Corps developed, it was plain to see,
Courage, endurance, loyalty, and skill
To a morale firm as morality,
Hardening him to an instrument, until

The finitude of virtues that were there
Bodied within the swarthy uniform
A compact innocence, childlike and clear,
No doubt could penetrate, no act could harm.

When he stood near the Russian partisan
Being burned alive, he therefore could behold
The ribs wear gently through the darkening skin
And sicken only at the Northern cold,

Could watch the fat burn with a violet flame
And feel disgusted only at the smell,
And judge that all pain finishes the same
As melting quietly by his boots it fell.

A Map of the City

I stand upon a hill and see
A luminous country under me,
Through which at two the drunk must weave;
The transient's pause, the sailor's leave.

I notice, looking down the hill,
Arms braced upon a windowsill;
And on the web of fire escapes
Move the potential, the gray shapes.

I hold the city here, complete:
And every shape defined by light
Is mine, or corresponds to mine,
Some flickering or some steady shine.

This map is ground of my delight.
Between the limits, night by night,
I watch a malady's advance,
I recognize my love of chance.

By the recurrent lights I see
Endless potentiality,
The crowded, broken, and unfinished!
I would not have the risk diminished.

The Byrnies

The heroes paused upon the plain.
When one of them but swayed, ring mashed on ring:
   Sound of the byrnie's knitted chain,
Vague evocations of the constant Thing.

   They viewed beyond a salty hill
Barbaric forest, mesh of branch and root
   —A huge obstruction growing still,
Darkening the land, in quietness absolute.

   That dark was fearful—lack of presence—
Unless some man could chance upon or win
   Magical signs to stay the essence
Of the broad light that they adventured in.

   Elusive light of light that went
Flashing on water, edging round a mass,
   Inching across fat stems, or spent
Lay thin and shrunk among the bristling grass.

   Creeping from sense to craftier sense,
Acquisitive, and loss their only fear,
   These men had fashioned a defense
Against the nicker's snap, and hostile spear.

   Byrnie on byrnie! as they turned
They saw light trapped between the man-made joints,
   Central in every link it burned,
Reduced and steadied to a thousand points.

Thus for each blunt-faced ignorant one
The great gray rigid uniform combined
    Safety with virtue of the sun.
Thus concepts linked like chain mail in the mind.

    Reminded, by the grinding sound,
Of what they sought, and partly understood,
    They paused upon that open ground,
A little group above the foreign wood.

---

byrnie—chain mail
nicker—water monster

Considering the Snail

The snail pushes through a green
night, for the grass is heavy
with water and meets over
the bright path he makes, where rain
has darkened the earth's dark. He
moves in a wood of desire,

pale antlers barely stirring
as he hunts. I cannot tell
what power is at work, drenched there
with purpose, knowing nothing.
What is a snail's fury? All
I think is that if later

I parted the blades above
the tunnel and saw the thin
trail of broken white across
litter, I would never have
imagined the slow passion
to that deliberate progress.

"Blackie, the Electric Rembrandt"

We watch through the shop front while
Blackie draws stars—an equal

concentration on his and
the youngster's faces. The hand

is steady and accurate;
but the boy does not see it

for his eyes follow the point
that touches (quick, dark movement!)

a virginal arm beneath
his rolled sleeve: he holds his breath.

. . . Now that it is finished, he
hands a few bills to Blackie

and leaves with a bandage on
his arm, under which gleam ten

stars, hanging in a blue thick
cluster. Now he is starlike.

The Feel of Hands

The hands explore tentatively,
two small live entities whose shapes
I have to guess at. They touch me
all, with the light of fingertips

testing each surface of each thing
found, timid as kittens with it.
I connect them with amusing
hands I have shaken by daylight.

There is a sudden transition:
they plunge together in a full-
formed single fury; they are grown
to cats, hunting without scruple;

they are expert but desperate.
I am in the dark. I wonder
when they grew up. It strikes me that
I do not know whose hands they are.

Rastignac at 45

Here he is of course. It was his best
trick always: when we glance again toward
the shadow we see it has consist-
ed of him all along, lean and bored.

We denounced him so often! Yet he
comes up, and leans on one of the bars
in his dark suit, indicating the
empty glass as if we were waiters.

We fill it, and submit, more or less,
to his marvelous air of knowing
all the ropes debonair weariness
could care to handle, of "everything

that I know I know from having done,
child, and I survive." What calmly told
confidences of exploration
among the oversexed and titled,

or request for a few days' loan, are
we about to hear? Rastignac, tell us
about Life, and what men of your
stamp endure. It must be terrible.

It is. To the left of his mouth is
an attractive scarlike line, not caused
by time unhelped. It is not the prize,
either, of a dueler's lucky thrust.

But this: time after time the fetid
taste to the platitudes of Romance
has drawn his mouth up to the one side
secretly, in a half-maddened wince.

We cannot help but pity him that
momentary convulsion; however,
the mere custom of living with it
has, for him, diminished the horror.

My Sad Captains

One by one they appear in
the darkness: a few friends, and
a few with historical
names. How late they start to shine!
but before they fade they stand
perfectly embodied, all

the past lapping them like a
cloak of chaos. They were men
who, I thought, lived only to
renew the wasteful force they
spent with each hot convulsion.
They remind me, distant now.

True, they are not at rest yet,
but now that they are indeed
apart, winnowed from failures,
they withdraw to an orbit
and turn with disinterested
hard energy, like the stars.

IV

Misanthropos

to Tony Tanner and Don Doody

THE LAST MAN

I

He avoids the momentous rhythm
of the sea, one hill suffices him
who has the entire world to choose from.

He melts through the brown and green silence
inspecting his traps, is lost in dense
thicket, or appears among great stones.

He builds no watch tower. He lives like
the birds, self-contained they hop and peck;
he could conceal himself for a week;

and he learns like them to keep movement
on the undipped wing of the present.
But sometimes when he wakes, with the print

of stone in his side, a relentless
memory of monstrous battle is
keener than counsel of the senses.

He opens, then, a disused channel
to the onset of hatred, until
the final man walks the final hill

without thought or feeling, as before.
If he preserves himself in nature,
it is as a lived caricature

of the race he happens to survive.
He is clothed in dirt. He lacks motive.
He is wholly representative.

I I

At last my shout is answered! Are you near,
Man whom I cannot see but can hear?

                                        Here.

The canyon hides you well, which well defended.
Sir, tell me, is the long war ended?

                                        Ended.

I passed no human on my trip, a slow one.
Is it your luck, down there, to know one?

                                        No one.

What have I left, who stood among mankind,
When the firm base is undermined?

                                        A mind.

Yet, with a vacant landscape as its mirror,
What can it choose, to ease the terror?

                                        Error.

Is there no feeling, then, that I can trust,
In spite of what we have discussed?

Disgust.

III

Earlier, traveling on the roads where grass
Softened the gutters for the marsh bird's nest,
He walked barefoot already, and already
His uniform was peeling from his back.
And coming to this hill across the plain,
He sloughed it bit by bit. Now that, alone,
He cannot seek himself as messenger,
Or bear dispatches between elm and oak,
It is a clumsy frock he starts to fashion
From skins of mole and rabbit; he considers
That one who wears it is without a role.
But the curled darling who survives the war
Has merely lost the admirers of those curls
That always lavished most warmth on his neck;
Though no one sees him, though it is the wind
Utters ambiguous orders from the plain,
Though nodding foxgloves are his only girls,
His poverty is a sort of uniform.
With a bone needle he pursues himself,
Stitching the patchwork spread across his lap,
A courier after identity, and sees
A pattern grow among the disarray.

IV

The moon appears, distinct where all is dim,
    And steady in the orbit it must go.
    He lies in shadow, then light reaches him.
While, there! the Milky Way follows below,
    A luminous field that swings across the sky.
    The ancient rhythm almost comforts, slow
Bright mild recurrence that he might move by,
    Obedient in the act of breath, and lit,
    Mere life, by matter traveling sure and high.
But this is envy for the inanimate,
    The youth of things. On the dead globe he sees
    Markings as one might on the earth from it,
Where relics of emergent matter freeze.
    Down here, two more births followed on the first:
    Life, consciousness, like linked catastrophes.
Their sequence in him cannot be reversed
    Except in death, thus, when the features set.
    Meanwhile, he must live, as he looks, immersed
In consciousness that plots its own end yet;
    And since the plotter through success would lose
    Knowledge of it, he must without regret
Accept the inheritance he did not choose,
    As he accepted drafting for that war
    That was not of his choosing. He must use
The heaviness, the flaw, he always bore.
    The imperfect moon swims forward on its course;
    Yet, bathed by shade now, he imagines more—
    The clearest light in the whole universe.

V

Green overtaking green, it's
endless: squat grasses creep up,
briars cross, heavily weighed
branches overhang, thickets
crowd in on the brown earth gap
in green which is the path made

by his repeated tread, which,
enacting the wish to move,
is defined by avoidance
of loose ground, of rock and ditch,
of thorn-brimmed hollows, and of
poisoned beds. The ground hardens.

Bare within limits. The trick
is to stay free within them.
The path branches, branches still,
returning to itself, like
a discovering system,
or process made visible.

It rains. He climbs up the hill.
Drops are isolate on leaves,
big and clear. It is cool, and
he breathes the barbarous smell
of the wet earth. Nothing moves
at the edges of the mind.

MEMOIRS OF THE WORLD

VI

It has turned cold. I have been gathering wood.
Numb-fingered, hardly feeling what I touched,
Turning crisp leaves to pick up where I could
The damp sticks from beneath them. I have crouched
Piling them up to dry, all afternoon,
And have heard all afternoon, over and over,
Two falling notes—a sweet disconsolate tune,
As if the bird called, from its twiggy cover,
      Nót now, nót now, nót now.

I dislodge sticks for kindling, one by one,
From brambles. Struck by shade, I stand and see,
Half blinding me, the cold red setting sun
Through the meshed branches of a leafless tree.
It calls old sunsets to my mind, one most
Which colored, similarly, the white-gray, blackened
Iron and slabbed concrete of a sentry post
With its cold orange. Let me live, one second,
      Nót now, nót now, nót now.

Most poignant and most weakening, that recall.
Although I lived from day to day, too, there.
Yet the comparison makes me sensible
Of the diminishing warmth and light, which were,
Or seem to have been, diminished less than now.

(58)

The bird stops. Hardening in the single present,
I know, hearing wind rattle in a bough,
I have always harked thus after an incessant
      Nót now, nót now, nót now.

V I I

Who was it in dark glasses?
Nobody in the street could
see if my eyes were open.
I took them off for movies
and sleep. I waited, I stood
an armed angel among men.

Between the dart of colors
I wore a darkening and
perceived an exact structure,
a chart of the world. The coarse
menace of line was deepened,
and light was slightly impure.

Yet as I lingered there was,
I noticed, continual
and faint, an indecision,
a hunger in the senses.
I would devour the thin wail
of foghorns, or abandon

my whole self time after time
to the chipped glossy surface
of some doorjamb, for instance,
cramming my nail with its grime,
stroking humps where colorless
paint had filled faults to substance.

I was presence without full
being; but from the corner,
in the mere fact of movement,
was I entering the role
of spy or spied on, master
or the world's abject servant?

VIII

Dryads, reposing in the bark's hard silence,
Circled about the edges of my fire,
Exact in being, absolute in balance,
Instruct me how to find here my desire:

To separate the matter from its burning,
Where, in the flux that your composures lack,
Each into other constantly is turning.
In the glowing fall of ash—rose, gray, and black,

I search for meaning, studying to remember
What the world was, and meant. Therefore I try

To reconstruct it in a dying ember,
And wonder, does fire make it live or die?

And evil everywhere or nowhere, stealing
Out of my reach, on air, shows like a spark.
I think I grasp it. The momentary feeling
Is merely pain, evil's external mark.

The neighboring cinders redden now together,
Like earlier worlds to search, where I am shown
Only myself, although I seek another,
A man who burnt from sympathy alone.

I X

A serving man. Curled my hair,
wore gloves in my cap. I served
all degrees and both sexes.
But I gave readily from
the largess of high spirits,
a sturdy body and strong

fingers. Nor was I servile.
No passer-by could resist
the fragrant impulse nodding
upon my smile. I labored
to become a god of charm,
an untirable giver.

Needing me, needing me, "Quick!"
they would call: I came gladly.
Even as I served them sweets
I served myself a trencher
of human flesh in some dark
sour pantry, and munched from it.

My diet, now, is berries,
water, and the gristle of
rodents. I brought myself here,
widening the solitude
till it was absolute. But
at times I am ravenous.

            X

All that snow pains my eyes, but I stare
on, stare on, lying in my shelter,

feverish, out at the emptiness.
A negative of matter, it is

a dead white surface at random crossed
by thin twigs and bird tracks on the crust

like fragments of black netting: hard, cold,
windswept. But now my mind loses hold

and, servant to an unhinged body,
becoming of it, sinks rapidly

(6 2)

beneath the stitched furs I'm swaddled in,
beneath the stink of my trembling skin,

till it enters the heart of fever,
as its captive, unable to stir.

I watch the cells swimming in concert
like nebulae, calm, without effort,

great clear globes, pink and white.—But look at
the intruder with blurred outline that

glides in among the shoals, colorless,
with tendrils like an anemone's

drifting all around it like long fur,
gently, unintelligently. Where

it touches it holds, in an act of
enfolding, possessing, merging love.

There is coupling where no such should be.
Surely it is a devil, surely

it is life's parody I see, which
enthralls a universe with its rich

heavy passion, leaving behind it
gorgeous mutations only, then night.

(6 3)

It ends. I open my eyes to snow.
I can sleep now; as I drowse I know

I must keep to the world's bare surface,
I must perceive, and perceive what is:

for though the hold of perception must
harden but diminish, like the frost,

yet still there may be something retained
against the inevitable end.

X I
Epitaph for Anton Schmidt

The Schmidts obeyed, and marched on Poland.
And there an Anton Schmidt, Feldwebel,
Performed uncommon things, not safe,
Nor glamorous, nor profitable.

Was the expression on his face
"Reposeful and humane good nature"?
Or did he look like any Schmidt,
Of slow and undisclosing feature?

I know he had unusual eyes,
Whose power no orders might determine,
Not to mistake the men he saw,
As others did, for gods or vermin.

For five months, till his execution,
Aware that action has its dangers,
He helped the Jews to get away
—Another race at that, and strangers.

He never did mistake for bondage
The military job, the chances,
The limits; he did not submit
To the blackmail of his circumstances.

I see him in the Polish snow,
His muddy wrappings small protection,
Breathing the cold air of his freedom
And treading a distinct direction.

ELEGY ON THE DUST

XII

The upper slopes are busy with the cricket;
　　But downhill, hidden in the thicket,
Birds alternate with sudden piercing calls
　　The rustling from small animals
Retreating, venturing, as they hunt and breed
　　Interdependent in that shade.

Beneath it, glare and silence cow the brain
　　Where, troughed between the hill and plain,
The expanse of dust waits: acres calm and deep,
　　Swathes folded on themselves in sleep
Or waves that, as if frozen in mid-roll,
　　Hang in ridged rows. They cannot fall,
Yet imperceptibly they shift, at flood,
　　In quiet encroachment on the wood—
First touching stalk and leaf with silvery cast,
　　They block the pores to death at last
And drift in silky banks around the trunk,
　　Where dock and fern are fathoms sunk.

Yet farther from the hill the bowl of dust
　　Is open to the casual gust
That dives upon its silence, teasing it
　　Into a spasm of wild grit.
Here it lies unprotected from the plain,
　　And vexed with constant loss and gain,
It seems, of the world's refuse and debris,

Turns to a vaguely heaving sea,
Where its own eddies, spouts, and calms appear.
    But seas contain a graveyard: here
The graveyard is the sea, material things
    —From stone to claw, scale, pelt, and wings—
Are all reduced to one form and one size.
    And here the human race, too, lies.
An imperfection endlessly refined
    By the imperfection of the mind.
They have all come who sought distinction hard
    To this universal knacker's yard,
Blood dried, flesh shriveled, and bone decimated:
    Motion of life is thus repeated,
A process ultimately without pain
    As they are broken down again.
The remnants of their guilt mix as they must
    And average out in grains of dust
Too light to act, too small to harm, too fine
    To simper or betray or whine.

Each colorless hard grain is now distinct,
    In no way to its neighbor linked,
Yet from wind's unpremeditated labors
    It drifts in concord with its neighbors,
Perfect community in its behavior.
    It yields to what it sought, a savior:
Scattered and gathered, irregularly blown,
    Now sheltered by a ridge or stone,
Now lifted on strong upper winds, and hurled
    In endless hurry round the world.

(67)

THE FIRST MAN

XIII

The present is a secure place to inhabit,
The past being fallen from the mind, the future
A repetition, only, with variations:
The same mouse on its haunches, nibbling, absorbed,
Another piece of root between the forefeet
Slender as wishbones; the wood lice, silvery balls;
The leaves still falling in vestiges of light.

Is he a man? If man is cogitation,
This is at most a rudimentary man,
An unreflecting organ of perception;
Slow as a bull, in moving; yet, in taking,
Quick as an adder. He does not dream at night.

Echo is in the past, the snow long past,
The year has recovered and put forth many times.

He is bent, looks smaller, and is furred, it seems.
Molelike he crouches over mounds of dirt,
Sifting. His eyes have sunk behind huge brows.
His nostrils twitch, distinguishing one by one
The smells of the unseen that blend to make
The black smell of the earth, smell of the Mother,
Smell of her food: pale tender smell of worms,
Tough sweet smell of her roots. He is a nose.
He picks through the turned earth, and eats. A mouth.

If he is man, he is the first man lurking
In a thicket of time. The mesh of green grows tighter.
There is yew, and oak picked out with mistletoe.
Watch, he is darkening in the heavy shade
Of trunks that thicken in the ivy's grip.

XIV

"What is it? What?"
Mouth struggles with the words that mind forgot.
    While from the high brown swell
He watches it, the smudge, he sees it grow
As it crawls closer, crawls unturnable
And unforeseen upon the plain below.

    "That must be men."
Knowledge invades him, yet he shrinks again
    And sickens to live still
Upon the green slopes of his isolation,
The "final man upon a final hill,"
As if he did a sort of expiation.

    And now he dreams
Of a shadowed pool nearby fed by two streams:
    If he washed there, he might,
Skin tautened from the chill, emerge above,
Inhuman as a star, as cold, as white,
Freed from all dust. And yet he does not move.

Could he assert
To men who climb up in their journey's dirt
    That clean was separate?
The dirt would dry back, hardening in the heat:
Perpetual that unease, that world of grit
Breathed in, and gathered on the hands and feet.

    He is unaware
Of the change already taking place as there,
    In the cold clear early light
He, lingering on the scorched grass wet with dew,
Still hunched but now a little more upright,
In picturing man almost becomes man too.

    XV

Hidden behind a rock, he watches, grown
As stony as a lizard poised on stone.
Below, the indeterminate shape flows steady
From plain to wood, from wood to slope. Already
Sharp outlines break, in movement, from the edge.
Then in approach upon the final ridge
It is slowly lost to sight, but he can hear
The shingle move with feet. Then they appear,
Being forty men and women, twos and threes,
Over the rim. From where he is he sees
One of the last men stumble, separate,
Up to the rock, this rock, and lean on it.

(70)

You can hear him gulp for wind, he is so close,
You can hear his hand rasp on the shriveled moss
Blotching the rock: by peering you can see
What a ribbed bony creature it must be,
Sweat streaking dirt at collarbones and spine,
Sores round the mouth disfiguring the line.

And on the thin chest two long parallel
Clear curving scratches are discernible.
Recent, for only now the drops within
Steal through the white torn edges of the skin
To mix with dirt. Round here, such cuts are common.
It is not hard to visualize the human,
Tired, walking upward on a wooded slant;
Keeping his eyes upon the ground in front,
He made his way round some dropped rotten limb,
And a hanging briar unnoticed swung at him.
And only later does it start to sting.
That wood has its own way of countering.
The watcher is disturbed, not knowing why.
He has with obstinate equanimity,
Unmoving and unmoved, watched all the rest,
But seeing the trivial scratches on the chest,
He frowns. And he performs an action next
So unconsidered that he is perplexed,
Even in performing it, by what it means—
He walks around to where the creature leans.
The creature sees him, jumps back, staggers, calls,
Then, losing balance on the pebbles, falls.

(71)

Now that he has moved toward, through, and beyond
The impulse he does not yet understand,
He must continue where he has begun,
Finding, as when a cloud slips from the sun,
He has entered, without stirring, on a field
The same and yet more green and more detailed,
Each act of growth discovered by his gaze;
Yet if the place is changed by what surveys,
He is surveyed and he himself is changed,
Bombarded by perceptions, rearranged—
Rays on the skin investing with a shape,
A clarity he cannot well escape.

He stops, bewildered by his force, and then
Lifts up the other to his feet again.

XVI

Others approach, and I grip
his arm. For it seems to me
they file past my mind, my mind
perched on this bare rock, watching.

They turn and look at me full,
and as they pass they name me.

What is the name Adam speaks
after the schedule of beasts?

Though I grip his arm, the man,
the scratched man, seems among them,
and as he pauses the old
bitter dizziness hits me:
I almost fall. The stale stench!
the hangdog eyes, the pursed mouth!
no hero or saint, that one.

It is a bare world, and lacks
history; I am neither
his lord nor his servant.

By an act of memory,
I make the recognition:
I stretch out the word to him
from which conversations start,
naming him, also, by name.

XVII

Others approach. Well, this one may show trust
   Around whose arm his fingers fit.
The touched arm feels of dust, mixing with dust
   On the hand that touches it.

And yet a path is dust, or it is none,
   —Merely unstable mud, or weeds,
Or a stream that quietly slips on and on
   Through the undergrowth it feeds.

His own flesh, which he hardly feels, feels dust
    Raised by the war both partly caused
And partly fought, and yet survived. You must,
    If you can, pause; and, paused,

Turn out toward others, meeting their look at full,
    Until you have completely stared
On all there is to see. Immeasurable,
    The dust yet to be shared.

The Goddess

When eyeless fish meet her on
her way upward, they gently
turn together in the dark
brooks. But naked and searching
as a wind, she will allow
no hindrance, none, and bursts up

through potholes and narrow flues
seeking an outlet. Unslowed
by fire, rock, water, or clay,
she after a time reaches
the soft abundant soil, which
still does not dissipate her

force—for look! sinewy thyme
reeking in the sunlight; rats
breeding, breeding, in their nests;
and the soldier by a park
bench with his greatcoat collar
up, waiting all evening for

a woman, any woman
her dress tight across her ass
as bark in moonlight. Goddess,
Proserpina: it is we,
vulnerable, quivering,
who stay you to abundance.

No Speech from the Scaffold

There will be no speech from
the scaffold, the scene must
be its own commentary.

The glossy chipped
surface of the block is like
something for kitchen use.

And the masked man with his
chopper: we know him: he
works in a warehouse nearby.

Last, the prisoner, he
is pale, he walks through
the dewy grass, nodding

a goodbye to acquaintances.
There will be no speech. And we
have forgotten his offense.

What he did is, now,
immaterial. It is the
execution that matters, or,

rather, it is his conduct
as he rests there, while
he is still a human.

Taylor Street

The small porch of imitation
marble is never sunny, but
outside the front door he
sits on his kitchen chair facing
the street. In the bent yellowish
face, from under the brim
of a floppy brown hat,
his small eyes watch what
he is not living. But he
lives what he can:
watches without a smile, with
a certain strain, the warmth
of his big crumpled
body anxiously cupped
by himself in himself, as
he leans over himself not
over the cold railing, un-
moving but carefully getting
a little strength from the sight of the
passers-by. He has it
all planned: he will live
here morning by morning.

Touch

You are already
asleep. I lower
myself in next to
you, my skin slightly
numb with the restraint
of habits, the patina of
self, the black frost
of outsideness, so that even
unclothed it is
a resilient chilly
hardness, a superficially
malleable, dead
rubbery texture.

You are a mound
of bedclothes, where the cat
in sleep braces
its paws against your
calf through the blankets,
and kneads each paw in turn.

Meanwhile and slowly
I feel a is it
my own warmth surfacing or
the ferment of your whole
body that in darkness beneath
the cover is stealing
bit by bit to break
down that chill.

You turn and
hold me tightly, do
you know who
I am or am I
your mother or
the nearest human being to
hold on to in a
dreamed pogrom.

What I, now loosened,
sink into is an old
big place, it is
there already, for
you are already
there, and the cat
got there before you, yet
it is hard to locate.
What is more, the place is
not found but seeps
from our touch in
continuous creation, dark
enclosing cocoon round
ourselves alone, dark
wide realm where we
walk with everyone.

Confessions of the Life Artist

"Whatever is here, it is
material for my art.

On the extreme shore of land,
and facing the disordered
rhythms of the sea, I taste
a summoning on the air.

I derive from these rocks, which
inhibit the sea's impulse.
But it is a condition,
once accepted, like air: air
haunted by the taste of salt.

II

I think, therefore I cannot
avoid thought of the morrow.
Outside the window, the birds
of the air and the lily
have lost themselves in action.
I think of the birds that sleep
in flight, of the lily's pale
waxy gleaming, of myself,
and of the morrow pending.
The one thing clear is that I
must not lose myself in thought.

III

You control what you can, and
use what you cannot.
     Heady,
to hover above the winds,
buoyant with a sense of choice.
Circling over a city,
to reject the thousand, and
to select the one. To watch
the goodly people there, to
know that their blood circulates,
that it races as yours does,
live between extremities.

IV

But what of the unchosen?

They are as if dead. Their deaths,
now, validate the chosen.

Of course, being left as dead
may lead to the thing itself.
I read about them: and what
could be more fortifying
to one's own identity
than another's suicide?

If there are forbidden arts,
mine must indeed be of them.

(81)

V

She is immersed in despair,
but I am here, luckily.
She, become indefinite,
leans on me who am starkly
redefined at each moment,
aware of her need, and trained
to have few needs of my own.

As I support her, so, with
my magnificent control,
I suddenly ask: 'What if
she has the edge over me?'

VI

To give way to all passions,
I know, is merely whoring.
Yes, but to give way to none
is to be a whoremaster.

I stride through the whorehouse
when my girls are off-duty,
I load them with chocolates,
but cannot for one moment
possess red hair like hers, fresh
cheeks or bee-stung lips like hers,
or a wasteful heart like hers.

VII

I elevate not what I
have, but what I wish to have,
and see myself in others.

There is a girl in the train
who emulates the beehive
of the magazine stars of
four years ago.
                    I blush at
the jibes that grow inside me,
lest someone should utter them.

Why was something evolved so
tender, so open to pain?

VIII

Here is a famous picture.

It is of a little Jew
in Warsaw, some years ago,
being hustled somewhere. His
mother dressed him that morning
warmly in cap and cloth coat.
He stares at the camera
as he passes. Whatever
those big shining dark eyes have
just looked on, they can see now
no appeal in the wide world.

IX

I grow old in the design.

Prophecies become fulfilled,
though never as expected,
almost accidentally,
in fact, as if to conform
to some alien order.

But I am concerned with my
own knowledge that the design
is everywhere ethical
and harmonious: circles
start to close, lines to balance.

X

The art of designing life
is no excuse for that life.

People will forget Shakespeare.
He will lie with George Formby
and me, here where the swine root.
Later, the solar system
will flare up and fall into
space, irretrievably lost.

For the loss, as for the life,
there will be no excuse, there
is no justification."

In the Tank

A man sat in the felon's tank, alone,
Fearful, ungrateful, in a cell for two.
And from his metal bunk, the lower one,
He studied where he was, as felons do.

The cell was clean and cornered, and contained
A bowl, gray gritty soap, and paper towels,
A mattress lumpy and not overstained,
Also a toilet, for the felon's bowels.

He could see clearly all there was to see,
And later when the lights flicked off at nine
He saw as clearly all there was to see:
An order without color, bulk, or line.

And then he knew exactly where he sat.
For though the total riches could not fail
—Red weathered brick, fountains, wisteria—yet
Still they contained the silence of a jail,

The jail contained a tank, the tank contained
A box, a mere suspension, at the center,
Where there was nothing left to understand,
And where he must reenter and reenter.

Pierce Street

Nobody home. Long threads of sunlight slant
Past curtains, blind, and slat, through the warm room.
The beams are dazzling, but, random and scant,
Pierce where they end
                    small areas of the gloom
On curve of chair leg or a green stalk's bend.

I start exploring. Beds and canvases
Are shapes in each room off the corridor,
Their colors muted, square thick presences
Rising between
                  the ceiling and the floor,
A furniture inferred much more than seen.

Here in the seventh room my search is done.
A blue fly circles, irregular and faint.
And round the wall above me friezes run:
Fixed figures drawn
                  in charcoal or in paint.
Out of night now the flesh tint starts to dawn.

Some stand there as if muffled from the cold,
Some naked in it, the wind around a roof.
But armed, their holsters as if tipped with gold.
And twice life-size—
                 in line, in groups, aloof,
They all stare down with large abstracted eyes.

A silent garrison, and always there,
They are the soldiers of the imagination
Produced by it to guard it everywhere.
Bodied within
            the limits of their station
As, also, I am bodied in my skin,

They vigilantly preserve as they prevent
And are the thing they guard, having some time stood
Where the painter reached to make them permanent.
The floorboards creak.
            The house smells of its wood.
Those who are transitory can move and speak.

V

Rites of Passage

Something is taking place.
Horns bud bright in my hair.
My feet are turning hoof.
And Father, see my face
—Skin that was damp and fair
Is barklike and, feel, rough.

See Graytop how I shine.
I rear, break loose, I neigh
Snuffing the air, and harden
Toward a completion, mine.
And next I make my way
Adventuring through your garden.

My play is earnest now.
I canter to and fro.
My blood, it is like light.
Behind an almond bough,
Horns gaudy with its snow,
I wait live, out of sight.

All planned before my birth
For you, Old Man, no other,
Whom your groin's trembling warns.
I stamp upon the earth
A message to my mother.
And then I lower my horns.

Moly

Nightmare of beasthood, snorting, how to wake.
I woke. What beasthood skin she made me take?

Leathery toad that ruts for days on end,
Or cringing dribbling dog, man's servile friend,

Or cat that prettily pounces on its meat,
Tortures it hours, then does not care to eat:

Parrot, moth, shark, wolf, crocodile, ass, flea.
What germs, what jostling mobs there were in me.

These seem like bristles, and the hide is tough.
No claw or web here: each foot ends in hoof.

Into what bulk has method disappeared?
Like ham, streaked. I am gross—gray, gross, flap-eared.

The pale-lashed eyes my only human feature.
My teeth tear, tear. I am the snouted creature

That bites through anything, root, wire, or can.
If I was not afraid I'd eat a man.

Oh a man's flesh already is in mine.
Hand and foot poised for risk. Buried in swine.

I root and root, you think that it is greed,
It is, but I seek out a plant I need.

Direct me, gods, whose changes are all holy,
To where it flickers deep in grass, the moly:

Cool flesh of magic in each leaf and shoot,
From milky flower to the black forked root.

From this fat dungeon I could rise to skin
And human title, putting pig within.

I push my big gray wet snout through the green,
Dreaming the flower I have never seen.

For Signs

1

In front of me, the palings of a fence
Throw shadows hard as board across the weeds;
The cracked enamel of a chicken bowl
Gleams like another moon; each clump of reeds
Is split with darkness and yet bristles whole.
The field survives, but with a difference.

2

And sleep like moonlight drifts and clings to shape.
My mind, which learns its freedom every day,
Sinks into vacancy but cannot rest.
While moonlight floods the pillow where it lay,
It walks among the past, weeping, obsessed,
Trying to master it and learn escape.

I dream: the real is shattered and combined,
Until the moon comes back into that sign
It stood in at my birth hour; and I pass
Back to the field where, statued in the shine,
Someone is gazing upward from the grass
As if toward vaults that honeycomb the mind.

Slight figure in a wide black hat, whose hair
Massed and moon-colored almost hides his face.
The thin white lips are dry, the eyes intense
Watching not thing, but lunar orgy, chase,

Trap, and cool fantasy of violence.
I recognize the pale long inward stare.

His tight young flesh is only on the top.
Beneath it is an answering moon, at full,
Pitted with craters and with empty seas.
Dream mentor, I have been inside that skull,
I too have used those cindered passages.

But now the moon leaves Scorpio: I look up.

3

No, not inconstant, though it is called so.
For I have always found it waiting there,
Whether reduced to an invisible seed,
Or whether swollen again above the air
To rake the oubliettes of pain and greed
Opened at night in fellowship below.

It goes, and in its going it returns,
Cycle that I in part am governed by
And cannot understand where it is dark.
I lean upon the fence and watch the sky,
How light fills blinded socket and chafed mark.
It soars, hard, full, and edged, it coldly burns.

Three

All three are bare.
The father towels himself by two gray boulders,
    Long body, then long hair,
Matted like rainy bracken, to his shoulders.

    The pull and risk
Of the Pacific's touch is yet with him:
    He kicked and felt it brisk,
Its cold live sinews tugging at each limb.

    It haunts him still:
Drying his loins, he grins to notice how,
    Struck helpless with the chill,
His cock hangs tiny and withdrawn there now.

    Near, eyes half closed,
The mother lies back on the hot round stones,
    Her weight to theirs opposed
And pressing them as if they were earth's bones.

    Hard bone, firm skin,
She holds her breasts and belly up, now dry,
    Striped white where clothes have been,
To the heat that sponsors all heat, from the sky.

    Only their son
Is brown all over. Rapt in endless play,
    In which all games make one,
His three-year nakedness is everyday.

Swims as dogs swim.
Rushes his father, wriggles from his hold.
　His body, which is him,
Sturdy and volatile, runs off the cold.

　Runs up to me:
Hi there hi there, he shrills, yet will not stop,
　For though continually
Accepting everything his play turns up

　He still leaves it
And comes back to that pebble-warmed recess
　In which the parents sit,
At watch, who had to learn their nakedness.

Words

The shadow of a pine branch quivered
On a sunlit bank of pale unflowering weed.
I watched, more solid by the pine,
The dark exactitude that light delivered,
And, from obsession, or from greed,
Labored to make it mine.

In looking for the words, I found
Bright tendrils, round which that sharp outline faltered:
Limber detail, no bloom disclosed.
I was still separate on the shadow's ground
But, charged with growth, was being altered,
Composing uncomposed.

From the Wave

It mounts at sea, a concave wall
  Down-ribbed with shine,
And pushes forward, building tall
  Its steep incline.

Then from their hiding rise to sight
  Black shapes on boards
Bearing before the fringe of white
  It mottles towards.

Their pale feet curl, they poise their weight
  With a learn'd skill.
It is the wave they imitate
  Keeps them so still.

The marbling bodies have become
  Half wave, half men,
Grafted it seems by feet of foam
  Some seconds, then,

Late as they can, they slice the face
  In timed procession:
Balance is triumph in this place,
  Triumph possession.

The mindless heave of which they rode
  A fluid shelf
Breaks as they leave it, falls and, slowed,
  Loses itself.

Clear, the sheathed bodies slick as seals
    Loosen and tingle;
And by the board the bare foot feels
    The suck of shingle.

They paddle in the shallows still;
    Two splash each other;
Then all swim out to wait until
    The right waves gather.

The Garden of the Gods

All plants grow here; the most minute,
   Glowing from turf, is in its place.
   The constant vision of the race:
Lawned orchard deep with flower and fruit.

So bright, that some who see it near
   Think there is lapis on the stems,
   And think green, blue, and crimson gems
Hang from the vines and briars here.

They follow path to path in wonder
   Through the intense undazzling light.
   Nowhere does blossom flare so white!
Nowhere so black is earthmold under!

It goes, though it may come again.
   But if at last they try to tell,
   They search for trope or parallel,
And cannot, after all, explain.

It was sufficient, there, to be,
   And meaning, thus, was superseded.
   —Night circles it, it has receded,
Distant and difficult to see.

Where my foot rests, I hear the creak
   From generations of my kin,
   Layer on layer, pressed leaf-thin.
They merely are. They cannot speak.

This was the garden's place of birth:
   I trace it downward from my mind,
   Through breast and calf I feel it vined,
And rooted in the death-rich earth.

Flooded Meadows

In sunlight now, after the weeks it rained,
Water has mapped irregular shapes that follow
Between no banks, impassive where it drained
Then stayed to rise and brim from every hollow.
Hillocks are firm, though soft, and not yet mud.
Tangles of long bright grass, like waterweed,
Surface upon the patches of the flood,
Distinct as islands from their valleys freed
And sharp as reefs dividing inland seas.
Yet definition is suspended, for,
In pools across the level listlessness,
Light answers only light before the breeze,
Canceling the rutted, weedy, slow brown floor
For the unity of unabsorbed excess.

The Messenger

Is this man turning angel as he stares
At one red flower whose name he does not know,
 The velvet face, the black-tipped hairs?

His eyes dilated like a cat's at night,
His lips move somewhat but he does not speak
 Of what completes him through his sight.

His body makes to imitate the flower,
Kneeling, with splayed toes pushing at the soil,
 The source, crude, granular, and sour.

His stillness answers like a looking glass
The flower's, it is repose of unblown flame
 That nests within the glow of grass.

Later the news, to branch from sense and sense,
Bringing their versions of the flower in small
 Outward into intelligence.

But meanwhile, quiet and reaching as a flame,
He bends, gazing not at but into it.
 Tough stalk, and face without a name.

The Discovery of the Pacific

They lean against the cooling car, backs pressed
Upon the dusts of a brown continent,
And watch the sun, now westward of their West,
Fall to the ocean. Where it led they went.

Kansas to California. Day by day
They traveled emptier of the things they knew.
They improvised new habits on the way,
But lost the occasions, and then lost them too.

One night, no one and nowhere, she had woken
To resin smell and to the firs' slight sound,
And through their sleeping bag had felt the broken
Tight-knotted surfaces of the naked ground.

Only his lean quiet body cupping hers
Kept her from it, the extreme chill. By degrees
She fell asleep. Around them in the firs
The wind probed, tiding through forked estuaries.

And now their skin is caked with road, the grime
Merely reflecting sunlight as it fails.
They leave their clothes among the rocks they climb,
Blunt leaves of ice plant nuzzle at their soles.

Now they stand chin-deep in the sway of ocean,
Firm West, two stringy bodies face to face,
And come, together, in the water's motion,
The full caught pause of their embrace.

Sunlight

Some things, by their affinity light's token,
Are more than shown: steel glitters from a track;
Small glinting scoops, after a wave has broken,
Dimple the water in its draining back;

Water, glass, metal, match light in their raptures,
Flashing their many answers to the one.
What captures light belongs to what it captures:
The whole side of a world facing the sun,

Re-turned to woo the original perfection,
Giving itself to what created it,
And wearing green in sign of its subjection.
It is as if the sun were infinite.

But angry flaws are swallowed by the distance;
It varies, moves, its concentrated fires
Are slowly dying—the image of persistence
Is an image, only, of our own desires:

Desires and knowledge touch without relating.
The system of which sun and we are part
Is both imperfect and deteriorating.
And yet the sun outlasts us at the heart.

Great seedbed, yellow center of the flower,
Flower on its own, without a root or stem,
Giving all color and all shape their power,
Still re-creating in defining them,

Enable us, altering like you, to enter
Your passionless love, impartial but intense,
And kindle in acceptance round your center,
Petals of light lost in your innocence.

VI

The Bed

The pulsing stops where time has been,
    The garden is snowbound,
The branches weighed down and the paths filled in,
    Drifts quilt the ground.

We lie soft-caught, still now it's done,
    Loose-twined across the bed
Like wrestling statues; but it still goes on
    Inside my head.

The Night Piece

The fog drifts slowly down the hill
And as I mount gets thicker still,
Closes me in, makes me its own
Like bedclothes on the paving stone.

Here are the last few streets to climb,
Galleries, run through veins of time,
Almost familiar, where I creep
Toward sleep like fog, through fog like sleep.

The Corporal

Half of my youth I watched the soldiers
And saw mechanic clerk and cook
Subsumed beneath a uniform.
Gray black and khaki was their look
Whose tool and instrument was death.

I watched them wheel on white parade grounds.
How could the flesh have such control?
Ballets with symmetry of the flower
Outlined the aspect of a soul
Whose pure precision was of death.

I saw them radiate from the barracks
Into the town that it was in.
Girl-hungry loutish casanovas,
Their wool and webbing grated skin
For small forgettings as in death.

One I remember best, a corporal
I'd notice clumping to and fro
Piratical along my street,
When I was about fifteen or so
And my passion and concern was death.

Caught by the bulk's fine inward flicker,
The white-toothed smile he turned to all,
Who would not have considered him
Unsoldierly as an animal,
Being the bright reverse of death?

(1 1 3)

Yet something fixed outlined the impulse.
His very health was dressed to kill.
He had the acrobat's love of self
—Balancing body was his skill
Against the uniform space of death.

Sparrow

Chill to the marrow
pity poor Sparrow
got any change Sir
Sparrow needs change Sir

I stand here in the cold
in a loose old suit bruised and dirty
I may look fifty years old
but I'm only thirty

My feet smell bad and they ache
the wine's gone sour and stale in my pores
my throat is sand I shake
and I live out of doors

I shelter from the rain
in a leaky doorway in leaky shoes
and there is only pain
I've got left to lose

I need some change for a drink
of sweet wine Sir a bottle of sherry
it's the sugar in it I think
will make me merry

I'll be a daredevil then
millionaire stud in my right mind
a jewel among men
if you'll be so kind

The bastard passed me by
fuck you asshole that's what I say
I hope I see you cry
like Sparrow one day

The Outdoor Concert

At the edge
of the understanding:
    it's the secret.

You recognize not
the content of it but
the fact that it is
there to be recognized.

Dust raised
by vendors and dancers
shimmers on the windless air
where it hovers
as if it will never settle.

The secret
is still the secret

is not a proposition:
it's in finding
what connects the man
with the music, with
the listeners, with the fog
in the top of the eucalyptus,
with dust discovered on the lip

and then in living a while
at that luminous intersection,
spread at the center
like a white garden spider
so still
that you think it
has become its web,

a god existing
only in its creation.

Bringing to Light

powder, chunks of road, twisted
skeletal metal, clay
         I think
of ancient cities of bringing to light
foundations under the foundations

bringing a raft of tiny
cellars to light of day:
gold pocks in the
broad sunlight, craters
like a honeycomb bared

. .   . .   . .

In one cellar, a certain manikin
terribly confined
in his sweat and beard
went crazy as Bothwell.
In another, his jailer lived,
here are his shelves for
cup and smock. He was a jailer
so knew he was free.

. .   . .   . .

Every day the luminous tiers
of the city are filmed with a dust,
a light silt from foot and flesh
and the traveling mind.

. .   . .   . .

I have forgotten a picnic on a hill
in Kent when I was six, but
have a page of snapshots about it.
It still takes place, but in
a cellar I cannot locate.

There is a cellar, a cell, a cellular
room where a handsome spirit
of willfulness picnics with me
all day limber imaginary brother
dandling me between his feet
kissing my eyes and mouth
and genitals making me
all his own all day
                    as he is mine.

. .   . .   . .

But beneath the superior cellars
others reach downward
                        floor under
floor Babel reversed

Opening doors I discover
the debris of sorcery interrupted
    bone structures like experiments

fewer and fewer
joining each other in their origins

separate words return to their roots
lover and mother melt into
one figure that covers its face
nameless and inescapable

need arrayed like a cause

Achilles and Achelous the river god
he fought unite in person
and in name as the earlier
Achelous who precedes both

tress of the Greek's hair red-glinting
braids with thick river weed
the cell darkens with braiding
toward their common root
in the lowest the last the
first cavern, dark and moist
of which
            the foundations
are merely the Earth

. .   . .   . .

nothing
      but a faint
smell, mushroomy, thin
as if something
          even here
were separating from its dam

a separating
      of cells

Autobiography

The sniff of the real, that's
what I'd want to get
          how it felt
to sit on Parliament
Hill on a May evening
studying for exams   skinny
seventeen   dissatisfied
          yet sniffing such
a potent air, smell of
grass in heat from
the day's sun

I'd been walking through the damp
rich ways by the ponds
and now lay on the upper
grass with Lamartine's poems

life seemed all
loss, and what was more
I'd lost whatever it was
before I'd even had it

a green dry prospect
distant babble of children
and beyond, distinct at
the end of the glow
St. Paul's like a stone thimble

longing so hard to make
inclusions that the longing
has become   in memory
an inclusion

The Idea of Trust

The idea of trust, or,
the thief. He
was always around,
"pretty" Jim.
Like a lilac bush or
a nice picture on the wall.
Blue eyes of an
intense vagueness
and the well-arranged
bearing of an animal.
Then one day he
said something!
               he said
that trust is
an intimate conspiracy.

What did that
mean? Anyway next day
he was gone, with
all the money and dope
of the people he'd lived with.

I begin
to understand. I see him
picking through their things
at his leisure, with
a quiet secret smile
choosing and taking,
having first discovered

and set up his phrase to
scramble
that message of
enveloping trust.

He's getting
free. His eyes
are almost transparent.
He has put on
gloves. He fingers
the little privacies of those
who acted as if there
should be no privacy.

They took that
risk.
        Wild lilac
chokes the garden.

Yoko

All today I lie in the bottom of the wardrobe
feeling low but sometimes getting up
to moodily lumber across rooms
and lap from the toilet bowl, it is so sultry
and then I hear the noise of firecrackers again
all New York is jaggedy with firecrackers today
and I go back to the wardrobe gloomy
trying to void my mind of them.
I am confused, I feel loose and unfitted.

At last deep in the stairwell I hear a tread,
it is him, my leader, my love.
I run to the door and listen to his approach.
Now I can smell him, what a good man he is,
I love it when he has the sweat of work on him,
as he enters I yodel with happiness,
I throw my body up against his, I try to lick his lips,
I care about him more than anything.

After we eat we go for a walk to the piers.
I leap into the standing warmth, I plunge into
the combination of old and new smells.
Here on a garbage can at the bottom, so interesting,
what sister or brother I wonder left this message I sniff.
I too piss there, and go on.
Here a hydrant there a pole
here's a smell I left yesterday, well that's disappointing
but I piss there anyway, and go on.
I investigate so much that in the end
it is for form's sake only, only a drop comes out.

(127)

I investigate tar and rotten sandwiches, everything, and go on.

And here a dried old turd, so interesting
so old, so dry, yet so subtle and mellow.
I can place it finely, I really appreciate it,
a gold distant smell like packed autumn leaves in winter
reminding me how what is rich and fierce when excreted
becomes weathered and mild

                              but always interesting
and reminding me of what I have to do.

My leader looks on and expresses his approval.

I sniff it well and later I sniff the air well
a wind is meeting us after the close July day
rain is getting near too but first the wind.

Joy, joy,
being outside with you, active, investigating it all,
with bowels emptied, feeling your approval
and then running on, the big fleet Yoko,
my body in its excellent black coat never lets me down,
returning to you (as I always will, you know that)
and now

            filling myself out with myself, no longer confused,
my panting pushing apart my black lips, but unmoving,
I stand with you braced against the wind.

The Cherry Tree

In her gnarled sleep it
begins
      though she seems
as unmoving as the statue
of a running man: her
branches caught in a
writhing, her trunk
leaning as if in mid-fall.
When the wind moves
against her grave body
only the youngest twigs
scutter amongst themselves.

But there's something going on
in those twisted brown limbs,
it starts as a need
and it takes over, a need
to push
      push outward
from the center, to
bring what is not
from what is, pushing
till at the tips of the push
something comes about
               and then
pulling it from outside
until yes she has them started
tiny bumps
appear at the ends of twigs.

Then at once they're all here,
she wears them like a coat
a coat of babies,
I almost think that she
preens herself, jubilant at
the thick dazzle of bloom,
that the caught writhing has become
a sinuous wriggle of joy
beneath her fleece.
But she is working still
to feed her children,
there's a lot more yet,
bringing up all she can
a lot of goodness from roots

while the petals drop.
The fleece is gone
as suddenly as it came
and hundreds of babies are left
almost too small to be seen
but they fatten, fatten, get pink
and shine among her leaves.

Now she can repose a bit
they are so fat.
                    She cares less
birds get them, men
pick them, human children wear them
in pairs over their ears

she loses them all.
That's why she made them,
to lose them into the world, she
returns to herself,
she rests, she doesn't care.

She leans into the wind
her trunk shines black
with rain, she sleeps
as black and hard as lava.
She knows nothing about babies.